99 Things Teens Wish They Knew Before®… Turning 16

Your Guide To Staying On Track To Success

Zach Veach

with Lindsey Gobel

www.99-series.com

The 99 Series
600 Brunet
Montreal, QC H4M1X8
Canada
323-203-0548

The author has done his/her best to present accurate and up-to-
date information in this book, but he/she cannot guarantee that the
information is correct or will suit your particular situation.

This book is sold with the understanding that the publisher and the
author are not engaged in rendering any legal, accounting or any
other professional services. If expert assistance is required, the
services of a competent professional should be sought.

First published by The 99 Series 2011

Cover designed and Layout by **Ginger Marks**
DocUmeantDesigns *www.DocUmeantDesigns.com*

Copy Edits by **Dana Owens**

Distributed by DocUmeant Publishing

For inquiries about volume orders, please contact:

99 Book Series, Inc.
books@99-series.com

Printed in the United States Of America
ISBN-13: 978-0-9868084-6-3 (paperback)
ISBN-10: 0986808466

WORDS OF PRAISE

FOR…

---

99 Things Teens Wish They Knew Before®… Turning 16

"Not only is Zach Veach an amazing kid (for his accomplishments as a race car driver), his common sense advice to teens in his quick-read new book 99 Things Teens Wish They Knew Before Turning 16, *reveals a maturity and level-headedness beyond his years. Teens will enjoy the book knowing it's coming from someone like them, who understands them and the challenges that teens today face."*—**Alyse Rome, *Founder/President, Amazing Kids!***

DEDICATION

This book is dedicated to all teenagers with a dream! Always follow your dreams and keep moving forward. As long as you keep moving forward, you'll be one step closer to your goal!

CONTENTS

ABOUT THE 99 SERIES

The 99 Series is a collection of quick, easy-to-understand guides that spell it all out for you in the simplest format; 99 points, one lesson per page. The book series is the one-stop shop for all readers tired of looking all over for self-help books. The 99 Series brings it all to you under one umbrella! The bullet point format, which is the basis for all the 99 Series books, was created purposely for today's fast-paced society. Not only does information have to be at our finger tips... we need it quickly and accurately, without having to do much research to find it. But don't be fooled by the easy-to-read format. Each of the books in the series contains very thorough discussions from our roster of professional authors so that all the information you need to know is compiled into one book!

We hope that you will enjoy this book as well as the rest of the series. If you've enjoyed our books, tell your friends. And, if you feel we need to improve something, please feel free to give us your feedback at www.99-series.com.

Helen Georgaklis
Founder & CEO, 99 Series

FOREWORD

My name is Michael Andretti, and most people know me as a racecar driver. During my driving career, I led more than 6,000 laps and won 42 Indy races. Since retiring from driving and becoming a race team owner, I've seen more than 50 wins and my teams have won five championships.

As big as those numbers are, there's one statistic that's more important than all others, and that's "three"—as in "my three children." With two already through their teen years and one who will be hitting the teenage mark in a few short years, I've had some practice steering others toward adulthood.

As you're growing up, you can sometimes hit a few roadblocks. I didn't win every race, but I knew that in order to get onto the podium, I had to keep going. I had to practice. Giving up—

either on a rough road course or a hard class—isn't going to make you any better than when you started. Quite often, it's those roadblocks that teach you valuable lessons.

When I started racing, I was a lot like Zach: young, determined, and ready to soak up all the knowledge I could. That's a big part of why I was so eager to sign Zach to our team. He understands the drive it takes to become a successful racecar driver, but can also deal with the pressures he will endure along the way. I hope I can help him get through some of the rougher patches by sharing my experiences.

In order to succeed in what you want to do, you have to work hard. That is one thing my father taught me, and I passed down to my kids. Even with a last name like "Andretti," no one is going to just hand you success. You have to work for it; lots of time in the gym, early wake-up calls at the track, and countless hours working to understand how the car runs. Zach will go through it all, just like I did in my racing days. Giving 100 percent is the only way to succeed.

Finding balance, at any point of your life, can be difficult. As a team owner, I spend a lot of time at the race track and even more time in the office working on the business side. But it's also important to spend time with family and friends. I make time to spend with my children outside of my racing life. As a teen, it's important to study hard and spend time with friends.

This industry is all about keeping your friends close. Over the years, I've made a conscious effort to surround myself with people I can trust. Sometimes, that means the crew that keeps my drivers safe while racing and other times, it means business associates who have the same drive for success as me. I've encouraged my son, Marco, to develop a close group of friends. They travel to his races, help keep him calm during stressful times and give him perspective when things don't go the way he had hoped. You need friends who will stand by you, whether you're in the spotlight or not.

As a dad, Zach's chapter "Dealing With Parents" definitely hit home. Though it may not always seem like it, your parents are always looking out for your best interests. They were in your shoes at one time; dealing with the same pressures and similar problems. Don't forget to thank them every once in a while.

My best advice to you is to do what you love. For Zach, Marco, others and me, it's racing. For you, it could mean preparing for college or practicing a craft. There's no better time than now to race toward your dream.

This book contains much of the same advice I've given to my own children for life, both on and off the race track. Unfortunately, there isn't an owners' manual for parenting. Nor has there ever really been one on how to get through your teen years. However, Zach has done a great job creating a road map for teens within the pages that follow. He's a smart young guy that has already been through a lot of things and he's willing to share some notable insight with you.

Enjoy <u>99 Things Teens Wish They Knew Before Turning 16</u> and begin your race toward a great time in your life!

Michael Andretti

ACKNOWLEDGMENTS

First, I want to thank my dad for giving up his dream, so I could start chasing mine. I can't thank you enough for always pushing me to be better and for your never-ending support. I can always count on you to be at my side, on the plane or the grid. It's comforting to know you'll be there throughout my life.

Second, thanks to the world's greatest mom! I want to thank you for always being there for me and taking care of my dog. I will never be able to thank you enough for being the loving and caring mom who always keeps me safe and makes me laugh!

To the rest of my family: thanks for being my biggest fan club and always checking on me when I'm on the road. I am proud to call you mine!

My teammate Sage Karam: thanks for a great year! You taught and pushed me to be a better driver and I can't wait to work with you again. You're my best friend and I can always count on you to have my back.

My Mentor Michael Andretti: thank you for giving me the chance of a lifetime and the realization of a dream fulfilled. I can not thank you enough for not only being my team owner but also for being a great mentor. Your advice is indispensable.

JF Thorman: thank you for making the call to invite me to Andretti Autosport and the kindness and support you gave to Sage and I last year. Your level of professionalism is incredible and drives me to be the most professional person I can be.

My USF2000 team: Ron Weaver, AJ Smith, Scott Graves, and Dave Popielarz, thank you for working hard every weekend and babysitting two teenagers every race weekend. You guys are my second family!

All the staff at Andretti Autosport, thank you for all your help and support! It is an honor to be part of such a great organization.

Dave Fisher: thank you for seeing an opportunity in me and helping develop my race craft.

To FocusDriven and Jennifer Smith: it's an honor to be your national spokesperson and to be a part of such a great organization. Together, I believe we can change the world and, more importantly, save lives!

To Oprah, for developing a platform, the "No Phone Zone," to expose the dangers of distracted driving to the nation and for helping to save lives, I offer my gratitude. The "No Phone Zone" has over 400,000 pledges, with more and more people signing everyday!

Klint: I can't thank you enough for molding my career and image. You have helped make me who I am and for that, I am forever grateful. I have had a blast working with you this past year and I'm excited to see what we can accomplish in the years to come!

Lindsey: It has been great working with you over the last year. I really appreciate all your help with the book. Without Klint's and your assistance, I wouldn't have realized my goal of writing this book!

Zach Veach

Thank you to my co-author, Zach Veach, for being a great partner and an amazing model for young adults. I am confident your stories and advice will help other teens follow your positive example.

Thank you to the 99 Series for involving me in another satisfying project.

Thank you to Zach's brand manager, Klint Briney. You are my perfect compliment in business and someone I have grown to regard as family. You are an impressive talent and I feel blessed to get to watch you achieve everything you deserve.

To my partner in life, Kyle: Without your support, I would not have the life of which I've always dreamed. Thank you for making everything possible and for encouraging me to be the best I can be. You make me incredibly happy.

To my mom and dad, Richard and Sue O'Connor: I don't know what I did to deserve you. I thank my lucky stars for you and for you giving me the best sister, and friend, in Kerry. You all make me feel very fulfilled and grateful.

Finally, to all of my friends and family: Thank you for understanding when I have to check out of life for a while and work on a project. Thank you for your patience and for not being upset with me when I don't return phone calls, or even know what day of the week it is. I love you all.

Lindsey Gobel

CHAPTER 1

GETTING YOUR LICENSE

#1: Practice, Practice, Practice

I have a special license, called an IMSA (International Motor Sports Association), which allows me to race cars. Yet, I only turned sixteen in December 2010. At last, I finally have my Ohio driver's license! Just like training for a race on a simulator, I have to practice driving a regular car before I will be a safe driver on the highways.

Driving a regular car is completely different than driving on the race track. Plus, everyone is going in different directions out in the real world. For example, there is even more than one way to turn left. You can make a hard-left or a soft-left; sometimes you get a green arrow, sometimes not. It can get very complicated.

One thing that always helps is practice. Going out with your parents or a safe adult-driver when you have your learner's permit can make getting your license much easier. Just practicing maneuvering the car through a parking lot can be helpful. It takes time to adjust to being in control of a moveable machine. Even figuring out how soon to start pressing the break before a red light takes some practice. My dad takes me to parking lots or back roads to get me used to being behind the wheel of a regular car. Just remember, every little bit helps.

Danica Patrick is a professional racecar driver in the IZOD IndyCar Series and NASCAR Nationwide Series. In 2005, she became the first woman to lead the famed Indianapolis 500 and holds the highest finish for a woman in its 94-year history. In 2008, when she took the checkered flag at Twin Ring Motegi, she became the first female to win a major closed-course auto race. She has been voted Favorite Female Athlete at the Nickelodeon Kids' Choice Awards, been named to Forbes "Most Powerful People in

Sports" list, and Time Magazine's "100 World's Most Influential People." Patrick shares her thoughts on the importance of practice:

The phrase, 'practice makes perfect' is a really great saying, but it can be misleading at times. The term 'perfect' is one that I don't necessarily like, because there is no such thing as perfect. Nevertheless, I do believe that practice makes you better than you would be without it, but to say it can make you the perfect racecar driver is unrealistic. No one will ever be a perfect racecar driver–but that doesn't mean you should ever stop trying to be one. We are all good at something; the challenge is to find out what 'it' is. Apply yourself and see what you are capable of becoming. When I first started go-karting I couldn't even keep up on the parade laps; even when the field was going about 1/10th of the speed! My dad kept on telling me 'laps, laps, laps' (which really meant: practice, practice, practice). So, we went out to the track as much as possible and I got better and better until I got to the point where I could compete. I am so glad I pushed myself and found my passion. Now, what is yours?

#2: Listen to Oprah!

Driving any vehicle is complicated enough without adding the extra distractions of talking on the phone or texting while driving.

Many of you have been following Oprah Winfrey's "No Phone Zone" campaign to keep our cars phone-free and our streets safe. It is a nationwide effort by Oprah and Harpo Studios to honor victims of distracted driving, while encouraging the American public to end deadly driving habits.

This is such an important issue to me that I stood before the Ohio House of Representatives to get a bill passed to ban distracted driving. I also released a Droid® application, urTXT, that alerts friends that you are driving and will get back to them. Download yours today in the Marketplace for Droid!

Using your phone while driving impacts driver-responsiveness as much as driving while intoxicated. The National Highway Traffic Safety Administration (NHTSA) reported that in 2008, almost 6,000 people were killed in crashes involving distracted driving. More than half a million were injured. Was that call or text message really that important? Most of us can agree that being on the phone while driving is not worth ending anyone's life.

I asked 33 drivers who raced in the Indy 500 to join me in signing Oprah's pledge to make our cars No Phone Zones. I think race car drivers are especially aware of the focus it takes to get behind the wheel. As professionals, showing our support for this cause is a responsibility we take seriously.

If you have recently obtained your driver's license, or will be soon, I ask you to follow the examples of IndyCar drivers like Danica Patrick, Helio Castroneves, and Tony Kanaan, personalities like CNN's Anderson Cooper, host of TLC's Trading Spaces' Paige Davis, and reality star Kim Kardashian, along with more than 400,000 others and counting (roughly equivalent to the entire audience at the Indianapolis 500) who have signed the pledge. Make your car a "No Phone Zone." Together we can put the brakes on this growing epidemic.

#3: Cruising With Friends

Phones aren't the only distraction in a car. When driving around with friends, you can be just as preoccupied. Whether you are messing with the music or trading stories with your passengers, it is easy to lose focus.

As an early driver who just got my license, I know how quickly I can get distracted by the radio or by my friends while I'm driving. If you do choose to drive with company, make sure that your first focus is always your driving. Set up your iPod® or CD before you start to drive and let your friends play DJ once you're on the move.

Just think about how horrible you would feel if you weren't paying attention and something bad happened. I would feel terrible if I wasn't paying attention and one of my friends got hurt. Think about this when you are joyriding with your crew.

When I race, it is easier for me to maintain focus because I'm the only one in the car. Off the track, I have to remember not to get distracted by all the additional factors that are involved when I'm driving with other people. Remember to stay focused and responsible. Avoid pressure to do otherwise.

#4: Watch the Weather

Driving conditions can change minute by minute, especially if you live in the Midwest like I do. A sunny day can bring thunderstorms without warning. Those previously dry conditions can turn slick in an instant.

Remember that tires react differently to roads when they are wet, dry, hot, or cold. You should practice driving in each of these different conditions. This way, you'll know when to take extra caution behind the wheel.

While riding on the interstate with my dad one evening, it began to rain. Immediately, my dad knew to slow the car slightly to accommodate for changes in the road conditions. The next thing I knew, I saw this truck speed by on our left. I can remember saying to my dad, "Man, that guy is going to hurt someone!"

Seconds later, the truck slid on the slick pavement, spun around so that they were facing our car, and slid sideways into the guardrail on our right.

We called the police to let them know there had been an accident and to come help the driver and passenger of the truck. Everyone was okay, but it could have easily been a lot worse.

Note: Roads are slickest when it first begins to rain. If the driver of that truck had slowed down when the weather changed, he could have avoided a potentially fatal accident.

#5: Put on Your "Away Message"

In addition to getting a bill passed in Ohio to ban distracted driving, I released a phone application called urTXT for the Droid® phone to send an automatic response to people trying to reach you when you're driving.

The new phone app can be activated and deacti- vated. It returns a text message to the sender, telling them that you are driving and will text them back later. This will give us a safe way to return texts while we are in the car, while keep- ing our communication timely. The app comes with pre-set messages or you can create your own.

So there's no need to jump when you hear that little noise your phone makes when you get a text. Remember that nothing is so urgent that we should endanger the lives of others.

#6: My Mission

One of the main reasons I decided to get involved to stop distracted driving is because of something that happened in my hometown: A 16-year-old girl pulled out in front of a tractor-trailer and was killed. She had been texting when the accident happened.

I couldn't stop thinking about it. Not only was this accident literally close to home, but I kept thinking about all of my friends and how we would all have our licenses soon. I didn't want to see the same thing happen to them because they were on their phone in the car or texting one of us while driving.

This young girl shouldn't have died. Her tragedy could have been prevented if she knew more about the dangers of distracted driving. That is when I decided to make it my personal mission to spread the word and do everything I could to prevent this from happening to anyone else.

#7: Buckle Up

The easiest thing you can do to protect yourself, in case of an accident, is to wear your seatbelt. Most states in the U.S. have laws that will force you to pay a fine if you get caught in a car without your seatbelt. That ticket also damages your driving record.

According to statistics, males between the ages of 16 and 25 are more likely to forego seatbelts than any other demographic. Let me just clear something up for the fellas; you will not look cool flying through a windshield.

Ryan Hunter-Reay is a professional racecar driver for Andretti Autosport in the IZOD Indy-Car Series. He won the IndyCar Series Rookie of the year award in 2007 and won his first IndyCar Series race at Watkins Glen International Raceway. Hunter-Reay shares his thoughts on the importance of buckling up:

Wearing your seat belt is a must. You don't have to be driving 220 miles an hour, like I do, to need your seat belt. If you're not wearing a seat belt, you can get seriously hurt; even in a crash where you're only going 25 miles an hour. Why take that risk?

Trust me; it's not smart and it's not cool. Putting on my seatbelt is a habit for me. It's the first thing I do when I get into any car I drive. Buckle up.

#8: Slow Down

So many people speed when they are running a little late, believing they will get to their destination sooner.

I heard about a study done on speeding in which researchers tested to see if speeding really got people to their destinations faster than those going the speed limit. The results proved that speeding didn't help travelers arrive any sooner than the rest of traffic. Plus, any time you drive a car over 60 miles per hour (mph), you use more gas. I don't know about the rest of you, but my allowance barely keeps up with gas prices these days! I certainly can't afford to waste money. A speeding ticket can cost you points and a hefty fine.

#9: Defensive Driving

Cars are getting bigger and bigger. With so many more distractions for drivers than ever before, being out on the road can be very scary. You can't rely on everyone to be as knowledgeable as you are about the dangers of using cell phones while driving. Nor is everyone sharing the road with you a good driver.

You need to be a defensive driver. Expect that someone around you will make a wrong move. Being ready to react and being prepared will help you to be alert and responsive when something out of the ordinary happens.

Be aware of your surroundings. Know where to go if something happens. Is there enough room on the shoulder of the road to swerve onto if the car next to you accidentally drifts over into your lane?

Sometimes people don't look before they change lanes. You need to be aware of cars around you, so that you can avoid accidents that happen as a result of others' carelessness.

Check out the intersection before you hit the gas when the light turns green. Sometimes people run red lights; they speed through the intersection even when your light has turned green. Just like crossing an intersection on foot, look both ways. Wait to make sure it is safe before you pull out.

Think about what could happen and be ready for those occurrences. That will make you a defensive driver and keep you and your car out of accidents.

Tony Kanaan is a professional racecar driver in the IZOD IndyCar Series and Indianapolis 500. He won the 2004 Indy Racing League's IndyCar Series championships points battle driving the 7-Eleven sponsored car. The Brazilian-born driver is the only driver to lead the Indianapolis 500 in each of his seven starts. Kanaan shares his thoughts on defensive driving:

> *Zach is correct. You must be prepared for the drivers around you to do something wrong. If you are only prepared for them to do the right thing, you are actually not prepared for anything. Put yourself in a safe position. Give yourself an 'out' and know what your next move is, should another driver do something dangerous. Always think one step ahead and keep an eye on all corners of your car. Check your mirrors often, and always be aware of what is going on around you.*

CHAPTER 2

LEADING A HEALTHY LIFESTYLE

#10: Input Equals Output

What you put into your body has a direct correlation to what you are able to get out of it. Driving a racecar is hard work. It takes lasting power and my body can't last if I don't fuel it with the things I need to stay in the race.

During your teen years, you form eating habits that will follow you through to adulthood. While your body is much better at processing and getting rid of unhealthy foods, the choices you make now will be ones that you will either maintain when you are older, or you will have to work hard to correct. I have to admit that I like to start my day with a hearty breakfast of … soda, but I can see a big difference in my performance on track when I take the time to eat and get some healthy food in my body.

I can get up for early morning media and grab a quick soda to get me jump-started, but I will find myself crashing around noon if I don't put something in my body that it can use.

From watching and listening to other racecar drivers and friends, I know that our bodies really begin to change around the ages of 18 and 19. Our metabolism slows and the foods we could eat with no problems before begin to take longer to process f. After that, they start getting stored as fat. If you, like most teenagers, are in the habit of eating fast food every day, you'll start to notice it affecting your body. So, if you practice good eating habits and keep junk food to a minimum early on, then your body will experience fewer physical changes when you reach those ages.

#11: Maintaining Your Vehicle

Workout habits are just like eating habits: the routines you get in now will be ones you are able to keep as an adult. Getting your body used to certain physical activities is like programming your iPod® to play your favorite song at a certain time each day. Your body will get so used to being maintained that after a while, it won't feel like work.

Because I'm small in stature, I really enjoy lifting to tone and build muscle. I also enjoy doing a lot of cardio exercises, like running. It gives my body the endurance to last during a race, like when I have to overpower a moving vehicle.

Try different activities to find out what you like to do. There are always groups and organizations in every city that offer classes or teams for fun and healthy competition. I love to compete. It's a great way to learn how to not only be a gracious winner, but a good loser as well.

At the age of 15, Kaylee Marie Radzyminski started an organization to support the troops called Tunes 4 the Troops. Tunes 4 the Troops collects new and used CD's, DVDs, and books on CD for the troops serving overseas. Radzyminski is a CNN Hero (Young Wonder) and named to the Washington Post's annual list of the 'Top-5 Leaders Under 30'. She has also been awarded over $150,000 in college scholarships.

Radzyminski shares her thoughts on maintaining your vehicle:

THINK: *Age 16 is a turning point in the lives of many young people. It is the beginning to a whole new world of responsibility. This responsibility could be directed towards a car, a cell phone or even saving money for the latest trend that all of your friends have. I know it may be hard to believe, but there is more to life than all that. What about college? Have you started thinking about what you want to be? Or how you will get there? It is never too early to start thinking and preparing.*

PREPARE: *Although my vehicle doesn't have four wheels or a roof, it has gotten me to where I am today. My vehicle is called 'Tunes 4 the Troops'. Throughout high school, I was constantly thinking about where I was going to attend college and what major I would choose. Planning the path for my life did not take a lot out of my day, or keep me from having fun. It did, however, prepare me and give me a great map for my future.*

DO: *I had an idea to help others. It was so simple; easy, in fact. Who doesn't have some extra CDs or DVDs lying around? Well, the* *next thing I knew, I was touching lives and inspiring tens-of-thousands of other young people all over the world! WOW! All because I started to DO something and, more importantly, I followed through. I found that when I was applying for schools I was also applying for scholarships. Because of my community service involvement with Tunes 4 the Troops, I was awarded over $150,000 in scholarship money. There are tons of scholarships available for people who are involved in community service. You are the future leaders of this great nation. Remember, it is never too early to start thinking, preparing and taking the actions that will get you to where you want to go.*

ENJOY: *Because of my hard work and maintaining my 'Tunes 4 the Troops' vehicle, along with thinking and preparing for college at an early age, I am now attending college on a full scholarship. I don't have to work or worry about student loans. I can focus on school and my education. I am enjoying the benefits of my hard work. No matter what roadblock came into view and even when it was hard, I kept going. That perseverance has shaped me into the person I am today. My mom always told me to reach for the stars. I didn't listen. Instead, I* *put my pedal to the metal and now Pluto is in my rear view mirror.*

#12: Don't Forget to Treat Yourself

Leading a healthy life doesn't mean giving up everything yummy. Foods like ice cream and candy might not be the best things for our body, but they are good for the soul. Allowing yourself treats every now and then actually helps you maintain a healthy lifestyle. Denying your body the foods you crave will just cause your body to rebel and binge! This could lead to over-consumption of bad foods and even make you sick. Balance is the key to a healthy diet.

My favorite food is pizza. If I took it completely out of my diet, I would go nuts and end up pigging out on it eventually. Letting myself have the junk foods I enjoy every now and then makes me feel like I am not punishing myself. And it makes choosing healthy foods, along with the occasional treat, easier. We don't have to eliminate things we like from our lives to be healthy, we just have to enjoy them in moderation.

#13: Just Say No Way

The last thing you want to put in your vehicle is something that is harmful. You would never put soda in your gas tank; that would ruin your car. So, why would you ever put drugs in your body?

I know a lot of us feel pressure from our friends to do things which may be uncomfortable. Just remember that there is only one person you need to look at in the mirror at the end of the day. Be true to that person and you will not only be able to make the best choices for you and your body, but you will be an example of confidence and individuality to others. Good behaviors are just as contagious as bad ones.

#14: With a Little Help from My Friends

Being around people who lead healthy lifestyles makes it easier to make good choices for your own life. Join a team or group that participates in healthy living, like sports or scouts. This will give you the encouragement you need to keep up those good habits. Building comradeship with people who share your interests and lifestyle will help you achieve your goals and make healthy living easy.

#15: Give a Little, Get a Lot

Roger Veach is my father and the best example of the kind of man I want to be. He gave up his dream so that I could pursue mine, and he is my biggest champion and ally:

> *Zach is the kind of kid who is always doing something to help someone else. From his work with the Oprah campaign to prevent more deaths from distracted driving, to seeing someone on the street and giving them whatever he has, Zach always thinks of others' needs before his own.*
>
> *I can remember, when he was in third grade, Zach asked his mom and me for money to attend a field trip. We gave him what he needed and then, a few days later, he asked us for the money again.*
>
> *I thought, "What did this kid do; blow all the money on baseball cards and video games?"*
>
> *It turned out one of his classmates didn't have the money to go on the trip, so Zach gave him his money. I think that is the best example of what kind of person Zach is and it's one of the qualities I love most about him. -Roger Veach*

#16: Championing a Cause

Alexander Hamilton said, "Those who stand for nothing fall for anything." I believe it's important to figure out where we stand on issues and support those we believe in.

That's how I got involved in my latest project to stop distracted driving. I saw a problem and knew I could do something to help. Sometimes I think it is easy to get discouraged when we see things happening in the world. We feel like we have no control or that our efforts couldn't possibly make a difference. Olivia Bouler would disagree.

Bouler is an 11-year-old girl who was upset over the recent damage to wildlife caused by the Gulf Coast oil spill that's been on every news station across the country lately. She decided to make watercolor paintings of birds that are local to that region to sell in an effort to raise money for the National Audubon Society, a group that rescues birds affected by the spill. Bouler has already raised tens of thousands of dollars for the cause and her efforts even got her noticed by America Online (AOL) News. They not only featured

Bouler on their website, but also made a hefty donation of $25,000 to the cause.

Olivia says that, "No matter what age, weight, height, or gender, people can change the world with whatever talent they possess."

Each one of us has the power to make a huge difference in this world and if we believe in something, we should do everything we can to see just how far our reach can go.

What kind of changes would you like to see?

#17: Staying Disease-Free

While this is a gross thing to talk about, it's an important subject to include when discussing leading a healthy lifestyle. Even if you're not having sex, you can still get diseases like herpes and other unattractive STDs if you engage in sexual activities. I learned in health class that you can get disgusting sores on your mouth and in your throat from oral sex. Yuck. It is important to be safe and think about the choices we make in the heat of the moment. Just think if you did something without thinking that led to a lifetime of dealing with a disease. Imagine how you would feel if there was a chance of you passing it on to your kids one day.

A mentor once told me to imagine being with my future wife. Would I be ashamed to tell her of my past experiences, or would I want to be a guy she could respect? Right now we might not be thinking about long-term things like that, but I would rather not be regretting at 30 what I did when I was 15.

#18: Following the Leaders

I like to look to my favorite IZOD IndyCar Series drivers, like Tony Kanaan, Helio Castroneves and Danica Patrick to get tips on healthy living. They are at a point in their careers that I am working towards. If we know what kind of end result we want, we can look to people who have achieved them and find out what it takes to get there.

It's always important to be your own individual and modify activities to fit your personal abilities and style, but it never hurts to get help from people who have been there. Why reinvent the wheel?

Alex Scott was a cancer patient who operated a lemonade stand to raise money to put an end to childhood cancer. She started "Alex's Lemonade Stand" in her family's front lawn, raising $1 million before the disease ultimately took her life at the tender age of eight. The Alex's Lemonade Stand Foundation was created to carry on Alex's work to cure all children with cancer by raising money and awareness for childhood cancer causes.

Alex was diagnosed with childhood cancer just before she turned one. She was paralyzed during her first surgery, on her first birthday. She worked hard for several years to learn how to walk, despite having significant paralysis in her lower extremities, as well as a lack of sensation in her legs.

When she was six years old, she had given up her walker and her leg braces and managed to walk around on her own; although not always steady and not quickly. Her dad suggested that she might try crutches. When she questioned why she would want them, he said so she could get around faster. Her response was, "Haven't you ever heard of the tortoise and the hare? Slow and steady wins the race."

Alex's logic is a great example of someone who believed in her abilities, even if they are different than everyone else's. She was confident that her way was just as good. And that's something we can all drink lemonade to!

CHAPTER 3

BULLYING

#19: How to Handle a Bully

Many racecar drivers have small body types; much like horse jockeys. There's not much room in the racecar, and we have to be in top physical condition to be able to hold on to the car for long periods of time. There is no room behind that wheel for excess weight. I'm no exception to that rule, which I guess made me an easy target at school.

One day, during health class, a rather large boy asked me if I was a "midget." Now, I know I'm small, but I'm hardly going to make the Guinness Book of World Records for my lack of height. I was completely thrown off-balance by his question. To make matters worse, the moment he chose to express his deep, intellectual thoughts about my body-type was in front of a room full of my peers, including one very cute girl I had only just worked up the nerve to say "hey" to on a regular basis.

This jerk had put me on the spot in front of the whole class. I didn't know how I was going to respond to his rudeness and come out the bigger man (pun intended). Then I thought about my parents. I thought about my mom, who was constantly filling my ears with things like, "Treat others the way you want to be treated," and "bringing yourself down to a bully's level, only makes two of you." Then I thought about my dad. He was on the small side when he was in school. He got picked on. Now he's not only a successful businessman with a great life and family, but he's someone I strive to be like every day.

So I told the guy, "No, I'm not a midget. I'm just small for my age. Maybe the issue is that you're a giant. Did you ever think of that?"

Not only did that stop him from turning our health class into his own personal quiz show, but he pretty much stayed away from me for the rest of the year.

#20: The Cyber Bully

Social networking is great for keeping in touch with my friends when I am out on the road for half a month at a time. I can Skype™ with my mom after a long day of practice and still feel close when I'm far away. But sometimes the things that bring us closer to the people we love also bring us closer to people who want to harm us.

By now, you should know to never post your location on Facebook or Twitter, or tell people when you'll be away from your house. Letting your friends know what you are up to is great, but posting your activities on the Web can also lead dangerous people right to you.

I'm sure you have heard about cyber bullying and how that can lead to tragedy. Oprah's friend, Dr. Phil, did a show on a case where a girl's mom and sister created a fake profile and pretended to be a boy another girl liked, so that they could bully her and say mean things to her online. The girl they were targeting ended up dying by suicide.

Bullies are everywhere and they are dangerous. Clearly, bullies aren't just our peers either. I think it is important that you reach out for help if you are approached by bullies. Whether you come across them in real life or online, you can find strength in numbers. Together, you can come up with a plan for how to deal with the bully before things go too far.

#21: Live to Fight another Day

Never engage in violence with a bully. Even if you are provoked, beating the crap out of each other won't change anything. Nor will it solve any problems. Bringing the issue to a physical level only increases the chance for disaster.

How many times have we seen something on television, where a person gets hit in a particular spot or their head hits the ground and they die? I remember hearing a story about two dads who got in a fight at a hockey game and one of them ended up dead; all over some stupid argument. Nothing is worth someone getting seriously hurt over or losing their life.

There is always an alternative to violence. If you don't know what to do, ask for help. Never hesitate to reach out when you feel like you are in over your head.

#22: You CAN Fight Back

I'm not saying you shouldn't defend yourself if someone is trying to hurt you. If someone is physically attacking you, you should fight back. My dad always tells me that I have every right to protect myself, but I think there are things we can do to prevent it from ever getting to that level.

Talking it over should always be your first step. If that doesn't work, bring in an outside party to settle the dispute. Whether it's a parent, teacher or just a neutral friend, sometimes getting a third perspective on the problem is just the ticket to solving the problem.

Sometimes, the bully is in your own house. Parents and relatives can also be bullies. It is important to know that we can get help, even if our own family members are the ones trying to take advantage of us. If the bully is a sibling or relative close to your age, you should talk to your parents or guardians to figure out how to handle the abuse.

If the bully is a parent, talk to other adults like teachers or counselors to figure out what to do.

#23: My Bully Wears Lipstick

I may be old fashioned, but I think that if you're a guy, it is never okay to hit or hurt a girl. Even if she hits you first, don't ever engage in anything physical with a girl. I'm not saying girls aren't as strong as boys, but I just don't think it is ever right, no matter the circumstances to participate in any kind of physical violence with a female; especially if you're a guy.

Girls can be just as intimidating as guys. If a girl is bullying you, she may just be trying to get your attention. Bullies' reasons for their behavior can be complicated and confusing. The best advice I can give anyone is to not react negatively to bullying from either gender. Talk to an adult about what's been going on and get some advice from someone who is more experienced in dealing with bullies.

#24: Girls Bullying Girls

Girls fight with one another totally different from guys. Guys have an argument, punch each other or wrestle for a bit, and the fight is over.

We never talk about it again. Girls are much craftier. Sometimes they go for the jugular. I have seen girls get angry with other girls and want to completely ruin someone's reputation over some stupid incident. And with social media and technology that allows us to spread something to millions of people in the blink of an eye, it is easy to do just that.

One thing all of us can do to help prevent this is to not buy into the bullying and rallying of sides by either party involved. Don't help to pass any information along, or re-post or listen to any rumor-spreading going on at school or online.

People say things out of anger; things that they will most likely wish they could take back later. We can help by not making things worse for the people fighting by adding fuel to the fire and passing along snarky comments or made-up stories about the people involved.

#25: Enough is Enough

When bullying gets out of hand or goes too far, it might be the time to let someone else handle the situation. If you have tried ignoring, befriending or just plain staying away from the bully and the situation is not getting any better, it is time to ask for help.

Think about what you would say to your best friend if they were in your situation. You would tell them to talk to their parents or teachers. Make them aware, so that they could put a stop to the behavior.

Sometimes, a bully will only respond to someone more powerful than they are, like a parent or teacher. If nothing you've tried works, it is time to call in the reinforcements.

We need to remember that even though they might do bad things, bullies are not bad people. They are probably just hurt and angry over something bad that happened to them. And, usually, our bullies have had someone bullying them at some point in their lives.

#26: Leave 'em Alone

No one deserves to be bullied. Even the biggest nerd in school doesn't deserve it. Think about it; their life is hard enough. They have already been labeled by others that they don't belong.

The loners who, one day, snap and completely lose it get to that point because they are either bullied their whole life or ignored. They might have had a chance at living a more normal life, had someone just taken the time to talk to them or reach out a helping hand. These are the people who usually can't defend themselves and are the easiest for bullies to target because they can't fight back. We should protect people who can't protect themselves.

No one needs their flaws pointed out, or to feel like they are not good enough. Don't we all feel that way? Making people feel better about themselves is the way to gain popularity. People want to be around people who make them feel good.

Picture your best friend or the person you like being around the most. I'll bet you like being with them because they make you feel good, or make you feel like a better version of yourself when you are around them. We should all try to be more like that. Strive try to be the person everyone likes to be around because you make them feel good about who they are.

Co-founder of Microsoft Bill Gates said, "Be nice to the nerds. Chances are, you'll end up working for one."

#27: Who Are Bullies, Anyway?

Bullies are usually people who are insecure about themselves. They pick on other people to take the focus off of the things they find embarrassing in their own lives. Try to remember that when someone is picking on you for no reason. Just tell yourself that you are not the one with the problem. Instead of being angry with the person, we should feel sorry for them and realize that they are the one that is really hurting. That's why they are acting out.

It's not easy to have that kind of perspective at any age, let alone as a teenager dealing with the pressures and problems of high school life. But keeping that information in the back of your head might just make you take a second to think before firing something back at a bully. This is not only a more mature reaction, but it also allows you to show everyone that you are a confident, together kind of person who doesn't need to prove anything. That right there will give you the advantage over any bully and will show everyone else what an awesome person you are.

CHAPTER 4

STUDY HABITS

#28: Making Lists

I probably travel more than your average tee-nager. I am on the road about half of every month during racing season. Trying to keep up with school and what I need to get done is some-times very hard. During the season, I wake up in a different city every few days.

What keeps me on track is writing everything down or putting it into my phone calendar. I have to keep lists of everything. If I didn't, I would miss important appointments or home-work assignments. That wouldn't show my par-ents that I am responsible enough to be a racecar driver.

Every day I make lists of the things I need to get done. That way, when I finish the task I can cross it off my list and I don't have to think about it again. (I have enough on my mind!) Also, crossing things off my list makes me feel like I'm accomplishing things and that makes me feel good.

When I feel like I am getting things done, it makes me feel like I can take on new challenges.

#29: Getting and Staying Organized

Some people have great memories. Someone can tell them something and they put it in a neat, little filing cabinet in their mind. Then, they can take it out whenever they need it. My mind probably looks more like my room, with stuff thrown everywhere. I have to dig a little more to find the things that I store in my memory. That's why it helps me to be well organized.

My room might be a mess, but when it comes to my schedule or stuff I have to do for racing, I take special care to be very organized. Besides making lists of the things I have to do, I keep and update a daily calendar to remember important events and appointments. If I need to get back to someone or turn something in to school on a particular day, I write a note in my calendar to remind me to get it done on time.

A published author, educator and literacy advocate, 12-year-old Adora Svitak began writing at the age of 4; publishing her first book, <u>Flying Fingers</u>, at the age of seven. Svitak teaches classes around the world, ranging in topics from language arts to leadership. She became the youngest person ever to speak at the TED conference in Long Beach, CA; joining speakers like former President Bill Clinton and Microsoft's Bill Gates. Svitak has been featured in numerous media outlets, including *The Oprah Winfrey Show* and *Good Morning America*. She shares her thoughts on staying organized:

> *When it comes to staying organized, sometimes you just have to go on the attack. I used to work on a large square desk. There was a little, tiny space for my laptop, and that was about it—everything else was covered in heaps of clutter. There were papers, Post-It notes, probably every kind of recyclable (but possibly cherished) possession I had. Finally, I decided enough was enough; I switched desks and set forth the decree that there would never, ever be a single thing on that desk, aside from my computer and a*

pencil jar. And my "obsessive" (and some-times aggressive) approach has worked! Not only is my family keeping their stuff off my desk, I am too. And that means I have more space to do the real work, instead of always cleaning.

#30: Study Methods

Everyone studies differently, because we all learn and remember in different ways.

Some people are visual learners. They can see a teacher write something on the board and they never forget it. Other people learn by repetition. Flashcards usually work well for these people. Writing facts down on index cards and repeatedly reviewing them will help them to remember information for a big test or quiz.

Another way to retain information is by writing it down. We remember a certain amount of information by reading it, a certain percentage more by writing down what we read (or the main points), and we remember a percentage more than that by reading it out loud, or by teaching it to someone else (even if it's just our dog).

#31: Your Workplace

It is important that the place in which you study or do homework is comfortable. It should not be too comfortable, like your bed or an overstuffed chair, because you don't want to fall asleep while you're working. It should be comfortable enough that you can concentrate. Our brains function better when they aren't distracted by an uncomfortable chair, or our legs are falling asleep because they aren't properly resting on the floor beneath us.

Sitting at a kitchen table or desk is the best place to study. You want to make sure you have time, without distractions, to work peacefully and allow yourself to concentrate on your homework or studies.

Mackenzie Bearup founded Sheltering Book, Inc., when she was 16 years old to provide books and open reading rooms for children in homeless shelters across the country. Bearup, who suffers from a very painful neurological condition called Reflex Sympathetic Dystrophy/Complex Regional Pain Syndrome, one of the most painful and least known neurological conditions, found that reading helped get her mind off of her pain.

To date, she has collected 43,000 books and provided libraries to homeless shelters in six states: Georgia, Illinois, Missouri, Tennessee, South Carolina and Kentucky. Bearup shares her thoughts on creating the right workplace:

Children are the future of this country and creating the right workplace to grow their minds as children is what will shape their future. On any given day, there are 1.35 million homeless children in the United States. Many of these children end up in homeless shelters; sometimes with a parent, but often times on their own—scared, worried and sad. Reading helped me escape my pain and worries and, from the beginning, I hoped that the books my organization provided would help other children escape their worries and emotional pains and create the right work environment to foster growth. Although I still suffer daily from Reflex Sympathetic Dystrophy, this doesn't stop me from doing the things I want to do. I live by my favorite quote: "Whether you believe you can do something or not, either way you are right." —Henry Ford.

#32: Find a Tutor

You can't be good at everything. We all need help mastering subjects that don't play to our strengths. At times like this it can be useful to get help from someone who is especially good at that subject. Getting help from a tutor can be a great way to clear up a subject that is confusing while boosting your Grade Point Average (GPA).

Talk to your parents about needing help. Usually, parents are more than willing to find their kids a tutor when they are having a hard time. It can be difficult for parents to know what you need if you don't tell them. If you are bringing home bad grades in a subject, they might think you are just lazy or slacking off. So letting them know that your struggle is not due to a lack of effort will show them that you are responsible. They can help find you a tutor, or you can ask your school to hook you up with one.

Most schools have lists of tutors available for every subject. Ask your teacher or guidance counselor for a list of tutors in the subject with which you need help. They will be happy to help you find the right tutor.

Teachers know it's sometimes difficult to provide the one-on-one help many students need when they have larger class sizes and a limited amount of time. Your teacher wants to help you succeed. They can and will help you find a tutor who can spend that time with you to help you better grasp the subject.

#33: Study Groups

Studying with classmates and friends can be a good way to retain information before a test. Sharing information can help to bridge gaps in the material or fill in notes that you might have missed in class. Plus, it can be easier to understand concepts when a friend or peer explains it, rather than a teacher.

It's amazing what you can accomplish and improve on when you are working with a group of people who have the same motivations and goals.

This should be done in addition to your regular studying, however. Don't rely on your study group for all of your studying. This method should be the last step in a series of habits that include re-reading the material, making notes, and studying alone. It is easy to get distracted in a group and lose focus on the most important information. You don't want that to be your only preparation for an exam.

#34: I'm Drowning in Homework!

Sometimes, it seems that I have so much homework that I can't decide where to begin. I start to feel overwhelmed and stressed out. When I start feeling like I have too much to do and not enough time to do it, I remind myself to take a step back, relax, and do one thing at a time.

I take a look at my list of things I have to do and when they need to get done. Then, I look at the things that have the shortest deadline and begin by knocking off the easiest things first. That way, I get the stuff that takes the least amount of time finished and crossed off my list. Now my list is much shorter and significantly less daunting.

#35: Distracted Studying

By now you know how opposed to distracted driving I am. Studying is no different. Our brains can only concentrate on so many things at once. When we overload our brain it cancels out the thing we need to be focused on the most.

Some of my friends argue that they can study just fine with the music blaring and television on. I don't buy it. When I'm watching MTV or VERSUS, I get so distracted by the programs that I can't focus on my math homework (my worst subject).

I have heard that music helps stimulate the brain. I can accept that listening to classical music (for example) at a reasonable level while doing homework could be a good thing. But I don't think that blasting heavy metal with the TV on while being logged on to Facebook or Twitter is going to do the trick. At least, it has never worked for me.

#36: Have a Snack

Another thing that can distract you from studying is your stomach. As an athlete, I have to pay attention to what my body needs. I have learned that when my most basic needs aren't being met, like sleep or hunger, it is hard to concentrate on anything else, let alone function at peak performance level.

When you get home from school it's a good idea to have a snack. Choose a snack without a lot of added sugar. You need something that will sustain you until dinnertime, so that you will be hungry for a good meal. Fruit is a great after-school snack. Apples, bananas and oranges have natural vitamins that give you the energy you need after a long day at school, without blasting your body with sugar and caffeine. Munching on healthy foods will sustain you between meals, while keeping your mind off of food. That way, when you begin studying or doing homework, your body can focus on what it needs to and not on the fact that it is hungry. Everyone knows that teenagers need to eat!

CHAPTER 5

DATING

#37: Getting Behind the Wheel

Asking questions shows we are interested in getting to know someone. Approaching a potential date is never easy. I try to remember that the most attractive quality I find in anyone is confidence. I know that if I appear confident, even when I feel insecure, it will make me more attractive to others. Confidence will allow you to take the first step to approaching anyone.

Talking to girls is not easy for me. I try to think about the things my mom has taught me. I also look to my older brother for clues. I have been told to treat girls with respect and to talk to them like I would talk to a good friend or someone I really care about. That helps me when I'm approaching a girl for the first time.

A good place to start is to say hello and ask them their name. Your next step might be a compliment. That way you are sure to start the relationship on a positive note. It also breaks the ice and gives you something to talk about.

#38: Ask Questions

If you spend the entire conversation talking about yourself, whether or not you realize it, you are telling the other person that you don't care about them. You also infer that you don't want to know anything about what makes them unique. I can't stand talking with people who just go on and on about themselves.

Ask people about their family and hobbies. This not only tells you a lot about the person and who they are, it also shows them your good intentions for the relationship.

#39: Have Fun

While movies like the "Twilight" series depict teen romances as full of serious drama, dating is actually really fun (in my opinion). This is the time in our lives where we are learning about each other and having a good time being fairly worry-free in our relationships. It's not the life or death situation we see on screen.

We don't need more pressures than we already have. My attitude is simple- I take life step-by-step and one day at a time. By not jumping ahead of myself, I get to enjoy where I am today.

#40: Know Your Speed Limits

As a teenager, your body is changing and your hormones are taking over. You are feeling and learning to deal with an entirely new set of emotions. Things can get heated up very quickly and it is easy to get lost in the moment.

Think about—and know—what your limits are ahead of time. That way, when the situation arises, you won't have to make decisions based on emotions. You will already know where you want things to stop and how far you are comfortable going. This will lessen the chance for regrets later.

#41: The Other "F" Word

Right now, we're at an age where we are trying to figure out the kind of person we want to be and who we really are. You, or someone you know, might be confused about sexuality or even afraid to be honest with friends and family about their feelings.

By now, you probably know someone who is gay. Older people might tell you that high school was the toughest time in their lives. We all know how scary it can be just being ourselves at this age. Imagine if you felt like people might make fun of you, or even try to hurt you, just for being who you are. You would be miserable.

None of my friends use gay slurs like the "F" word. I can tell you that they would not be my friends for long if they did. It is never okay to tease or make someone feel ashamed for who they love. Loving each other is a good thing. The people I look up to tell me it's something we should celebrate and embrace. It's never something we should make people feel bad about.

#42: Web Wars

Don't bring your fights to Facebook. This goes for any relationship, not just dating.

Never put private issues or conflicts online for everyone to see. Work out issues in person. Using the Web to rally support for your cause is a passive-aggressive way to handle an argument. Besides that, you are putting things in writing on the Web which you can't easily take back.

I see so many people on Facebook having arguments or disagreements with people who live in the same house. How does that make any sense? Why would you want other people to know what is going on in your personal life? Save that stuff to talk about with your close friends. Don't broadcast your problems to the world.

A lot of employers look at Facebook before they hire someone. It's really easy to type someone's name into a search engine and dig up any dirt that's been posted online. Remember that people are watching what you do and picture a potential boss looking over your shoulder as you type. What would you want them to read?

#43: What's Your Status?

Speaking of social networking sites, you might also think twice about changing your "status" online every time you begin or end a relationship.

Leaving that section blank allows you the freedom to date and break up with whomever you choose, whenever you want, without the added pressure of getting hundreds of inquiries from friends every time your status changes.

Unless the person you are dating is the person you plan to marry, you will be breaking up with them at some point; that is just a fact. Adding them to your online profile will only complicate things in the future.

#44: S-E-X

I'm not one of those people who feel like they have to take a stand on the issue of sex. I don't see myself as someone that others look to as their moral compass. It's a choice everyone has to make for themselves. My personal stance is a private issue—for me to know and not to broadcast to the world.

Nevertheless, I do think that it's something everyone should think long and hard about before deciding how they feel about it. I think you have to be mentally ready for something like sex; not just physically ready.

There are so many other issues that come along with having sex; so many things to think about. You have to think about protecting yourself against diseases, the possibility of pregnancy, and the millions of emotional issues that come along with bringing something like sex into a relationship. A person has to be ready to take responsibility for these potential end results before they decide they are ready for sex. If they are ready for all of that, then it should be a choice made by the two people involved.

#45: Answers

If you have questions about sex, or want to know more about how to protect yourself, talk to your parents, health teacher, or to a counselor. You can also get information from organizations like Planned Parenthood and your doctor's office.

Another option is the 99 Series book, <u>99 Things Parents Wish They Knew before Having 'THE' Talk</u>. It is a book that can provide you with answers to some of those uncomfortable questions.

CHAPTER 6

HIGH SCHOOL

#46: Enjoy

High School can be one of the best times of your life. Enjoy this time because soon you will have a lot more to worry about. One day you will have bills to pay and other people to take care of. You will have to stress over living life on your own. Before you have to move out of your parent's house and into the real world, take time to live it up worry-free for a while. Being in high school is really like being at your first job. In the beginning, you feel awkward because everything is new. But, as the years go on, you get more and more comfortable and fall into the swing of things.

Don't be intimidated by the newness of things. Eventually, those things will become routine and you will have forgotten what it was like to not know what you are doing. So many adults tell me that they wish they had high school to do all over again, knowing what they know now. I think they are talking about all the time we waste, worrying about the unknown.

The hardest thing about taking on a new challenge is that we don't know what to expect. If I can just remember to go in with the attitude that I'm going to know what I'm doing eventually, I don't worry so much about what to expect. I just expect that I'm going to master it.

#47: Sign Me Up

One of the best things about high school is that you get to try many new things to find out what you like to do or what you are good at. Most schools have a number of programs and teams in which you can get involved. It's a great way to challenge yourself and have some fun while making friendships that may last a lifetime.

My activity of choice is racing. That's where I spend all my time, and it is great to be a part of something I love doing. I love being around other people who love the sport as much as I do. Whether you're interested in sports or art, music or socializing, now is the best time to try your hand at different activities. This is your opportunity to find out what gets your engine going.

#48: Grades

With all of this fun stuff going on in high school, it's easy to forget that you have to get some work done too. Grades are important. If you want to go to college, reach your goals, and celebrate your win with the checkered flag of a fulfilled life, you have to make an effort in high school. Your grades are what colleges look at to determine if they will admit you.

A college doesn't want to take some kid with tremendous potential and bad grades. Colleges are businesses, and their graduates act as their report cards. They don't want you to attend if they have reason to think you will be a slacker and get bad grades. They want students who are going to participate, succeed, and make them look good. Getting good grades in high school just makes things easier for you down the road and gets you into good habits that will help you in college and in the workplace.

The best news is: it's never too late to start trying. If your grades aren't landing in the beginning of the alphabet, you can start turning them around, right now. Re-read the chapter on study habits and get back in gear.

#49: Teacher Trouble

Most of my teachers I have enjoyed having as instructors. Teachers are great people. Most of them teach because they really love teaching and are excited about their subject. But once, I had a teacher who just seemed like she was mad at the world. She was always in a bad mood. There was no pleasing her. She seemed to grade extra hard and her class was really tough for me.

While it was hard for me to understand at the time, when I finally got out of her class, I realized that I had become a better student. Being in her class made me work and try harder to get good grades. As a result I was smarter when I finished her class. You just have to remember that you are going to come across people who seem to make things difficult for you. Those people may be hard to deal with, but they will make you stronger because of the experience.

#50: Student Government

Sometimes there are things that go on in your school that you don't agree with, or you might feel like there is a better way of doing things. Student government is a great way to let your voice be heard. Your opinions might just help your school to make changes that could affect classes for years to come. It also looks great on your college applications to have been involved in something as important as the governing of your student body.

#51: Finding Your Style

These are the years when you are figuring out what your personal style is. We might experiment with different kinds of clothes or hairstyles to find which one fits us best. I try to remember that while I am still learning who I am, others are trying to figure out who they are as well. You need to respect that others need the freedom to try new things. Don't make fun of someone for the way they dress or some new style they are trying out. Clothes don't make the person. We are all unique in our own way and should be allowed to express our individuality in any form we choose.

#52: Who Are You Wearing?

I also remember and encourage others not to make fun of anyone who isn't wearing the latest styles or trends. Not everyone can afford to buy a pair of $200 jeans (I'd rather spend the money on car parts).

One of the IZOD IndyCar drivers I look up to is Sarah Fisher. In her book, <u>99 Things Women Wish They Knew Before Getting Behind the Wheel of Their Dream Job</u>, she says that people used to make fun of her in school for not having expensive clothes and shopping at thrift stores. Fisher went on to become the fastest woman on four wheels. I'm sure they aren't laughing now.

#53: Cafeteria Food

Like I mentioned in chapter two, the foods you put into to your body will determine how well it functions throughout the day. Choosing good foods at lunch will give us the energy we need to get through the rest of the school day, thus allowing our brain to retain the new information we get during the rest of our classes. While the ice cream and fries look good as we're going through the lunch line, they aren't going to help us when we're trying to do long-division.

#54: I've Got Spirit, How 'Bout You?

If you aren't an athlete or cheerleader, but you want to participate in school activities and show your school spirit, there are many other ways to support your school and teams. To support our classmates, we've painted our chests and made signs to hold up at games or pep rallies. If you're creative enough, don't be surprised if your sign makes it on ESPN's *SportsCenter*!

Tailgating can also be a lot of fun; cooking out with your friends before a game can become a tradition. Grilling burgers and chicken has become a fun pastime for us. If you're lucky, some of the players will swing by to grab a bite after the game.

If your school has a mascot, you can always try out to wear the costume during games and get fans pumped up. Or you can make up your own costume. Whatever your interests or talents, you can find a way to participate in school events and support your friends. And don't forget to show gratitude when your friends are supporting you at your events. It's amazing how much peer support means. It even gives you additional adrenaline when competing! Be sure they know how much you appreciate them.

CHAPTER 7

DRAMA

#55: Dealing With Emotions

Being a teenager sometimes comes with having to handle a roller coaster of emotions; at times, on a daily basis. Our lives are full of pressure from peers and parents, stress at school, and drama with our friends. It can be overwhelming and I know that sometimes, I feel completely out of control.

What helps me when I feel like all those things are taking over is talking to someone I trust. Whether it's a friend or my mom or dad, just getting whatever it is I'm worried about out in the open can make me feel better.

If that doesn't help, you can always talk to your school counselor, a religious figure or ask your parents to help you find a therapist. It may help to get feedback from someone who has an outsider's perspective on the problem.

Everyone has times in their life when they need help. If your leg was hurting you would go to the doctor, right? So why not ask for help from an expert when you feel like you can't handle an emotional problem?

Taylor LeBaron, 17, is a Ball Ground, GA, teen who went from 297 pounds to 145; a weight he's maintained for three years. At age 14, LeBaron took on his greatest challenge of overcoming his genetic predisposition to weight gain to develop a fitness plan based on video game strategies and changed his life. He penned his fitness plan and journey in his book, <u>Cutting Myself in Half: 150 Pounds Lost, One Byte at a Time</u>, and shares his thoughts on dealing with emotions:

> *Every time a friend hurts our feelings, a parent tells us they're proud of us, a teacher gives us a low grade, or that special person asks us to hang out with them, the result is an emotional feeling. If we don't laugh, cry,*

scream or otherwise release our emotions, they can build up in the form of stress.

People get rid of built-up emotional stress in all sorts of ways. But unfortunately, lots of us do so by overeating. But, whoa! That stress-fighting strategy puts on weight. I know from experience how stress-eating can add up. Overeating once helped me ac- cumulate 150 extra pounds.

I now deal with my emotions (a.k.a.–stress) by exercising. When I'm angry, I hop on a treadmill and run four or five miles. When I'm worried, extra strength-building exer- cises get my emotions back in check. The best thing about exercise is that it actually makes us healthier. So, when emotions start building up, try riding a bike, running, or even surprising Mom by cleaning the garage.

#56: What Is Depression?

You may have had or will have a time in your life when you felt completely helpless and didn't know how you were going to go on. Sometimes, just putting one foot in front of the other can seem like a challenge. Feeling sad, defeated, or worthless happens to all of us. But when it seems like we just can't shake it, or it is taking over our lives and keeping us from the people and things we love, then it is time to ask for help.

Talk to a loved one and let them know you are having a tough time and need a helping hand to get you out of this funk. Reaching out is the first step to getting your life back to normal and getting back to the things you enjoy.

#57: How to Get Help

If you're not ready to talk to someone you know, call an expert. 1-800-273-TALK is a lifeline. You can talk to someone who knows just how you feel and can give you tools to help get you through. It's free and the call is completely confidential.

Please don't ever be afraid to let someone know that you feel afraid or helpless. There are millions of people, all over the world, who have felt the same way you feel. As much as we all like to think we are different, the issues that we must tackle and the obstacles we face are all the same. There is always someone who has faced what you are going through. Take comfort in knowing that you are not alone and that others have overcome your struggle. You can overcome it, too. All you have to do is ask for help.

#58: Before Things Go Too Far

I recently found out that the amount of deaths by suicide is beginning to rival those of breast cancer. Yet, it's the single most preventable cause of death. You may have even thought about it or know someone who has attempted suicide. It is something we all need to be talking about.

Suicide accounts for more than 1 out of every 10 deaths among people between the ages of 15 and 24 each year. Don't let yourself or someone you know become just another statistic! Look for warning signs, like depression, and reach out for help.

Sometimes, it is hard to know when to tell someone if we have a friend who is showing signs of depression or could be suicidal. We might feel like they will get upset with us if we tell someone. But I would much rather have an angry friend than a dead one. Let someone know when you become worried about a loved one. Don't stop talking until they get the help they need.

#59: Cliques

One thing I don't miss about going to a regular high school is the cliques. The jocks hang out with the jocks, the popular girls have their group, the band kids stick together, and the rest of us just try to fit in where we can.

My friends are all different. Some of them really love music, others are good at sports, and some, like me, enjoy racing. I think it makes me well-rounded to not have friends in only one type of group. How boring would it be to hang out with people who only like the same things you do? You would never get to find out that there are other things you like too.

While you may tend to hang out with one partic-ular group in school, don't be afraid to branch out and make friends in other groups. You might be surprised to discover how much you have in common with your new friends.

#60: Celebrity Gossip

I don't know about the rest of you, but I am sick and tired of hearing every little detail about cele-brities' lives. Why are we so obsessed with knowing every last thing about them? What we are seeing is more and more of their flaws. We are learning that celebrities and athletes aren't the glamorous pictures of perfection we once believed them to be. But we are also losing our heroes.

Who are kids supposed to look up to? The greatest golfer in the world was just wrapped up in a scandal that completely ruined him in the eyes of some of his fans. If we could separate a person's private and professional lives, we wouldn't have to know all of their embarrassing characteristics or flaws. Don't we all want those things kept private?

If we all stopped paying attention to all the celebrity gossip, we would eventually stop getting bombarded with it every time we turn on the TV or look in a magazine.

#61: Sex-ting

You see public service announcements (PSAs) about it on TV. We may have even been told about or seen one for ourselves. Sex-ting is a dangerous game some teenagers are playing, and it can ruin our reputations and relationships.

Sending a sexy picture of yourself to someone else might seem like a good idea at the time, but how are you going to feel about it in six months? If the relationship ends are you going to be glad you did it? Will your picture get deleted? Probably not. Even if you trust the other person, it's just not a classy thing to do. Your next boyfriend or girlfriend won't appreciate that you did it and neither will you when your friends, and maybe even your mom and dad, find out about it.

One rule of thumb I use to decide if something is a good idea or not is something my mom says, "Picture your grandma standing next to you. Would you still do it? If the answer is no, then I would think twice about doing it."

#62: Take a Break

Sometimes drama can come from a fight with a friend, girlfriend, or boyfriend. If things get heated and you feel like you're not getting anywhere, taking a break to cool off might be the best solution. You can take the break apart or together. Either way it will give you the time, and perspective, to get out of the moment and calm down.

Take a walk around the neighborhood, or go out for ice cream. Try relaxing for a while or doing something to get rid of that negative energy. This will calm you down and help you to think clearly.

#63: Don't Start It

No one likes dealing with drama so if you can avoid it, don't be the one to start it. And, if your friends are having a fight, stay out of it as best you can. If you take sides and jump into their drama, you will be the one that gets blamed when they make up.

CHAPTER 8

AVOIDING PEER PRESSURE

#64: Stand Out from the Crowd

I'm a big fan of people who are individuals and don't subscribe to cliques. We're all much more interesting when we have our own style and flavor. I would much rather be unique than be like everyone else just so I could fit in.

Kids at school sometimes tease me for wearing my racing shirts to class. I like wearing them. You see, racing is a huge part of my life and I love everything about it. It is also what makes me unique.

The teasing never bothered me. Besides, when I didn't react and kept wearing my racing shirts, it showed them that I am confident enough to do what I want and be who I am. I think that is much cooler than dressing exactly like everyone else. Why not be a trendsetter yourself?

Winter Vinecki, 11, founded Team Winter at the age of nine to raise awareness and fund research for Prostate Cancer. A triathlete since age five, Vinecki talks about standing out from the crowd:

My dad, Michael, was diagnosed on his 40th birthday with prostate cancer and died before turning 41. For the past several years, Team Winter consisted of me racing by myself, raising money for prostate cancer research.

Realizing I could not do it alone, I expanded in 2010 to form a team of athletes across the world racing for Team Winter and Prostate Cancer Awareness; a concept similar to that of Susan G. Komen for the Cure® and Team in Training.

As the first ever Ambassador for IronKids, a youth triathlon series put on by Ironman, I serve as a role model to kids across America. I encourage them to lead an active, positive, and healthy lifestyle through the sport of triathlon. I also encourage them to race, not only for themselves, but for a cause dear to them.

With the help of many kids and adults, I have helped raise over $200,000 to fund research through the Prostate Cancer Foundation.

I have been told over and over again that 'I am too young;' too young to do an Olympic distance triathlon at age 9 (0.9 mile swim, 25 mile bike, 6.2 mile run, which I completed in under four hours), too young for a ½ marathon (13.1 miles) at age 10, which I completed in 1:52:03, 12 seconds shy from a 22 year-old course record, and too young for marathons (26.2 miles) which I will be doing before I turn 13.

While I have coaches and doctors who assure me everything I am doing is safe and not damaging to my body, I don't compete to show that I can. I know I can. I compete to show other kids and adults that anything is possible if we don't listen to those who tell us we can't.

I choose to stand out in honor of my dad and for the 1 in 6 men who will fight and/or fall victim to prostate cancer. I surround myself with family, friends, coaches, and athletes who believe in me and see me not as an age, but as an inspiration. My dad stood out as a young victim to prostate cancer. I am not afraid to stand out along side him.

#65: Communicate with Your Parents

When you are open and honest with your parents, they trust you to make your own decisions. Keeping them informed of what is going on in your life will not only keep you close, it will allow them to be there when you need them.

Your parents will never judge you. Sometimes what you may want to share may make you feel like you'll disappoint them or they'll disapprove. That's ok. It might sound lame, but our parents have been there. They can understand just how we feel, even when we feel like no one can. Talking with them will help us feel like someone's "got our back" when things get tough. Our parents will always love us no matter what.

#66: Got Faith?

Whatever you believe, you might think about getting involved in your church or religious group if you aren't already. It's nice to be able to talk to people who share your beliefs and have spiritual guidance from prominent figures within that community.

Knowing what we believe in makes difficult decisions easier. You also have people to go to if you feel like you can't talk to your parents, family, or friends about something.

#67: Your Gang

Keeping a diverse group of friends is a good way to avoid peer pressure. When all of your friends have different interests and activities, you are likely to avoid everyone jumping on the same bandwagon when something is a bad idea.

Being in a circle of good friends helps me to avoid getting stuck in a bad situation. I know that my friends aren't going to try to pressure me into doing something I don't want to do. My friends know who I am and wouldn't ask me to be any other way. I feel the same about them!

#68: Be Well-Rounded

While I love being behind the wheel of a racecar, it's not the only thing I do. I have a lot of interests. I play video games, I play with my dog, I go to movies with friends, and I'm involved in charity work.

Your community center usually offers sports and different activities in which you can become involved, either as a volunteer or as a participant. Learning to do something different can be really fun because you may have never known what you are capable of, until you try it.

Sometimes money can be an issue. Our parents may not be able to afford to let us join every sport or activity we are interested in, but there are always people and programs available that will allow you to be a part of something. The internet can be really helpful for keeping us informed with what is going on in our community.

When you have a lot of fun activities taking up your time, you are less likely to fall into bad habits as a result of peer pressure.

#69: Know Who You Are

If you feel like you are succumbing to peer pressure, take a step back and look at what you are doing. Does this seem like you? Are you happy with yourself at the end of the day? Would you feel comfortable if someone you admired saw you or found out what you are doing?

Most of our questionable choices can be figured out by simply imagining someone we respect standing next to us. Would we be proud of ourselves? If not, then it is a good idea to change the behavior or walk away from a situation.

Award-winning creator and founder of Pencil Bugs, Jason O'Neill was just nine years old when he became an entrepreneur. He has expanded into other products and is also a published author. Jason has received local and national media acclaim and been included on *Forbes* Top 10 List of Role Models 18 & Under, appeared on PBS *BizKid$* as well as other TV shows, and has been featured in many magazine and newspaper articles. He talks about knowing who you are:

> *As teenagers, we should not be expected to know who we are. We are still learning and trying to find who we are. At this point, our*

14 or 15 years are a small fraction of our entire life. Many things will change over our lifetime, including who we are or what we do.

However, by the time we are a teenager, we should know our core values, morals, what we stand for and what we believe. Zach mentioned the saying, "Those who stand for nothing fall for anything," by Alexander Hamilton, in point number 16 of this book.

As an entrepreneur who started a business at the age of nine, I have faced my share of challenges. Most of my peers could not relate to me. They did not understand what I was doing or why. It would have been easy to follow the crowd and not stick with my Pencil Bugs business. But, if you have strong values and believe in yourself, you can accomplish anything. Knowing who you really are will come with time.

#70: Call Your Lifeline

If you are in a situation you feel is dangerous, or could get you in trouble, you can always call for help.

I guarantee you that your parents will be less mad at you for calling them to get you out of a bad situation than if they found out about it on their own after the fact. It also shows them that you are responsible enough to know when you are in over your head and need help.

You'll build trust in your relationship with your parents and you will always have a safe ride home from wherever life takes you.

#71: Change of Scenery

If you feel like your group of friends is always pressuring you to do things that make you uncomfortable, then it is a good time to look for a change of scenery. Ditch those clones and find some friends that make you feel good to be around them.

Try taking up a new activity or hobby. My favorite hobby is going to my local R/C car track and racing with other people. You could also join an intramural sports team.

If you feel like you just can't get away from them, ask your parents if transferring schools is an option. It might be the chance for a fresh start you need.

#72: Good Peer Pressure

All peer pressure isn't bad. Sometimes our friends can influence us to make good decisions, too. Take my recent campaign with Oprah's "No Phone Zone" to prevent distracted driving. I've gotten 33 Indy 500 professional racecar drivers to sign Oprah's pledge to make their cars No Phone Zones.

When I approached Danica Patrick about signing the pledge, she seemed hesitant at first. She made me work for it and asked me lots of questions about the campaign. Finally, she looked to then-teammate Tony Kanaan and asked him if he had signed it.

Kanaan said, *"Of course I signed it; and you need to, too!"*

Thanks, Tony!

CHAPTER 9

DEALING WITH PARENTS

#73: Try to See It My Way

The first step to resolving any conflict, whether it's with your parents or friends, is to try to put yourself in the other person's shoes. Try to see their side of the argument. If you are upset with your parents because they won't take you somewhere, think about the reasons why they are telling you 'no.'

When you consider the other person's reasoning and point of view, you might agree with them or be able to find a reasonable solution. Like if the reason for not taking you somewhere is because you won't get home in enough time to cook dinner, suggest bringing home a pizza. They might go for it or they might not, but thinking about it from their side at least gives you a shot at getting what you want; or understanding why you can't.

#74: Think About It

Parents can be frustrating. Sometimes it seems like they don't understand us, or want us to have any fun. Other times, it seems like their nagging never ends.

I travel everywhere with my dad when I'm racing. I love my dad and look up to him, but sometimes I get frustrated with him. That is when I think about the reasons my dad is harping on me. He knows how bad I want this and how hard I work, and he wants me to be successful and see my dreams come true. If he can see something I can't that could help me out the next time, he is going to tell me about it, because he knows I want to be the best.

Thinking about the reasons behind why our parents do what they do might help us not to get so annoyed with them. After all, they are saying 'no' out of love.

#75: Time Out

Just like with our friends, sometimes we get into the heat of an argument with our parents. You go round and round without coming to any kind of resolution. Then it is best to take a moment and get away from the situation. Taking a few minutes to calm down, breathe, and think about what will allow us to come back to the conversation mellow and ready to find an answer.

If you continue an argument, then you are not offering a solution. More often than not, when we argue, it's because there is a problem that needs to be solved. Looking for a solution that you can all be come together on is far more beneficial than just arguing and getting nowhere fast. We are not always going to get our way.

Taking a time out gives everyone a chance to look at all sides. This can help us all come to some common ground.

#76: Getting Your Way

Another plus to the time out is that it gives us a chance to think about the argument objectively and reasonably. When we come back to our parents with a well-thought out plan of action or reasons to win our case, they are more likely to listen than if we just get angry and argue with them.

Parents respond to reason, not whining.

Casey Martin, 17, has a mission: to teach one million kids how to control their own emotions, attitudes, and choices. Known as "Calm Casey," he travels the country, speaking to 25,000 students each year through his "Straight Talk for Kids" school assemblies. Additionally, he has written and produced his own audio CDs, monthly newsletter and website, www.CalmCasey.com. During the summer, Casey runs an online "camp" to teach kids about making positive decisions. He shares his ideas about getting your way:

> *Like many of you, I have large dreams in life. But when I was younger, I got upset about everything my parents did. If my parents asked me do homework or chores, I'd get frustrated. If they made me go to the store, I'd throw a tantrum. If I couldn't find my video games, I would blame my parents. It seems like I was always battling my parents and trying to control them. That's when I realized that every time I reacted*

emotionally, I was giving those situations complete power over my happiness and destiny. I determined that in order to achieve my dreams, I had to stop trying to control my parents and instead, control myself.

This process works! When I began driving, I was tempted to stay out past my curfew and make an excuse. Instead, I came home 10 minutes early. By showing my parents that I could control myself, I built trust and they gave me more freedom. When my parents asked me to turn off my video games, I stopped negotiating and whining and said, "Okay, Mom." Here's the lesson: If you control yourself, your parents won't have to. And that gives you a lot of freedom and power. Because I can control myself, I now control my happiness and the course of my life. And you can, too!

#77: Stand-In

If you have a problem and you can't talk to your parents or feel like they aren't listening to you, talk to another adult outside of your home. This could be an aunt or uncle, a neighbor, or even another adult you admire. They might offer you perspective on why your parents aren't seeing things your way, or be able to help you come up with a plan to handle the situation.

#78: Take Your Medicine

If your parent loves you, then they will most likely punish you. For me, staying home from something I really want to do sometimes seems like the end of the world. It's not. Take your punishment like a champ and your parents will see you demonstrating responsible, adult behavior. They will see that you understand that there are consequences for your actions. This will give them faith that you have learned your lesson and will make better decisions in the future. Most likely, they will learn to trust you. And they might even let you off early for good behavior.

#79: Show 'em Some Love

I have heard some of my friends' parents talk about how they think their kids don't want them around. I think this is why some parents try to leave their kids alone when they are in the same house together. I guess they feel like their kid would rather be by himself/herself than hang out with them.

Sometimes parents need us to initiate things. Let them know you want them around. Try asking them how their day was, for a change. I guarantee you will see the reward. You can make your mom or dad's day by showing a little interest and letting them know you care.

Another great way to show them love is just to help around the house. Simply cleaning up the dishes after supper or putting our own laundry away can make all the difference to our parents. Showing love is not just a hug or saying, "I love you." Sometimes it is doing things that show your parents you really care about making them happy, too. Besides, the more you help out, the less nagging you get!

#80: Let's Play

One way to keep a good relationship with your parents (and to not get grounded) is to find an activity the whole family likes doing. I like playing video games with my parents and cornhole when it's nice outside. (That's a Midwest game. You toss beanbags through a hole in a wooden plank.) It's a great way to have fun and stay on your parent's good side.

Going for a walk or a bike ride together is good for the whole family, not only because you spend time together, but you exercise together, too. Keeping your parents active is good for them and helps them keep up with you.

#81: Bon Appetite

Eat dinner together. It's a great chance to unload your day and trade stories with the people you love the most.

Another fun way to get everyone together is to cook the meal as a family. Everyone gets a job and has fun getting dinner ready. Then, you all get to enjoy something you did together.

Pizza night is my favorite!

CHAPTER 10

CIRCLE OF FRIENDS

#82: Where to Find Them

Unless you go to school online like me, high school is the best place to meet other kids your age and make new friends. There are many groups you can get involved in at school. Spend time with people who share your interests, while building relationships and doing something you enjoy.

You don't have to already be good at something to get involved; just be interested. You may not be a good runner yet, but if you think you might enjoy joining the track team, go ahead and try out. They will teach you what you need to know and your skills will develop as you go along.

Meanwhile, you will get to know some new friends who are learning with you. You can help motivate each other while having fun along the way.

#83: Keep Your Friends Close

Having good friends means being a good friend. Show interest in your friends by finding out what is going on with them; and be a good listener.

I have to be away from my friends most of the time because of all of the traveling I do. Luckily, I can stay in touch with my friends through social networking and by talking to them on the phone or via Skype® while I am gone.

The best way to maintain and protect your relationships with your friends is to be someone they can trust and enjoy being around. Think about the qualities you look for in a friend and do your best to exhibit those characteristics yourself.

Be the kind of friend you'd want to have.

#84: Surround Yourself with Only the Best

Like it or not, we are judged by the company we keep. Think about it; if your parents started spending all of their time with shady-looking ex-cons, you might wonder what they were up to. Surrounding yourself with good quality friends not only ensures that you have a solid support system and great people to spend time with, it also reflects well on you and shows others what kind of person you are.

My parents love all of my friends. They take time to get to know who I am hanging out with. They know that they never have to worry about us because they know what kind of people we are. You get a lot more freedom when you show your parents that you and your friends are trust-worthy.

#85: Fights

In every relationship, you are going to come across speed bumps. There will be times when you aren't getting along with your friends. Just remember; working out our differences makes our relationships stronger. If we never fought, we would never have opportunities to learn about ourselves and grow.

The same thing happens in racing. When we crash, we learn a lot about the car and what adjustments we need to make. The next time we go out on the race track, we are smarter and have a better car to drive.

Our relationships only get better as we learn from our mistakes. Sometimes having little disagreements makes us better friends.

#86: Making Up

If you have a fight with your friends but after thinking about it, you realize that you are in the wrong, the best thing you can do is apologize. All any of us ever want to hear when we feel we've been wronged is, "I'm sorry," and, "I'm doing something to make sure it doesn't happen again."

Most of us are quick to forgive when someone gives us an apology. You can send your friend a nice note or gift, but an honest face-to-face apology is really the best way to get your friendship back on track.

#87: The One-Sided Friendship

Do you have a friend who always seems to be around when they need you, but is nowhere to be found when you need them? This is a one-sided friendship. They will treat you like their best friend when it is convenient for them, but they are all 'take' and no 'give' in the relationship. They only come around when they have a problem or things can be on their terms.

These are friends you should cut loose. They are only a drain on you, and you deserve better. All of us merit friendships that are back and forth; give and take. If it seems like your friendship is one-sided, then you should end it and spend that time with your true friends instead.

#88: How to Not Be THAT Guy (or Girl)

If you are worried that you might be in a one-sided friendship where YOU are the one doing all the taking from the relationship, take a step back and look at the facts:

- Is the other person always doing you favors?
- How often have you done something for them when they needed it?
- When you hang out with them, is it usually someplace you want to go and on your terms?

If you answered yes to all of these questions, you might be a bad friend. You can always turn it around, though. Next time you're hanging out, ask your friend what they want to do. If they are always giving you rides, offer them some gas money. Next time you catch a movie, let them pick the show. You will be a better friend and have more fun when the relationship is two-sided.

#89: When It's Over

Relationships end. Whether it is because classes are changing and you're around a new group of people every day or you just begin to grow in different directions, you can lose touch with friends.

This is just a normal part of getting older. I'm not interested in the same things I liked when I was 10, so I am not friends with the same people as when I was that age.

We have to let go of old friends to make room for new ones. People come in and out of our lives, but it doesn't make the relationship any less special if it ends.

#90: Three's a Crowd

Sometimes, when we're hanging out with friends, people can feel left out; especially if there are three of us. For some reason, two people at a time usually click better. This results in one person feeling like the outsider. If you are hanging out in a group of three, try to focus on both friends equally and not spend too much time with one or the other.

If you are the one being left out, try to jump into their conversation or activity instead of sulking because you feel ignored. When they see how much fun you are having, their attention will naturally drift back to you.

CHAPTER 11

PLANNING FOR COLLEGE

#91: Where to Go

I think a lot about where I want to go to college. Do I want to stay close to home? Do I want to get away? What do I want to study?

These are all good things to consider when picking your college. Talk to your parents and guidance counselor about what interests you. Your counselor can help guide you toward the best school. Your parents can take you to the college you are considering for a tour, where you can check out the campus and meet with people to learn more about the school.

Ask yourself what you are looking for. Are you into sports? Do you like music? Does a certain college offer more in one than the other? Keep your options open when you are choosing. It's important that you are comfortable with your decision. Just because your friends may be going to a specific school, it doesn't mean it will suit your needs.

#92: What Do I Want To Be When I Grow Up?

Talking to some of my older friends who have gone off to college has gotten me thinking that there is a lot of pressure to figure out what you want to do when you graduate from high school. Picking a college means making a decision that will affect the rest of your life.

It helps to consider what you think you might enjoy doing as a career. Then you can talk to your school counselor, teachers, family, friends, parents, or even people in that field about what kind of things you should be studying to get into that industry or sport.

You could also reach out to someone in the business and ask them for tips. Maybe you can do a summer internship to get your foot in the door or to find out if it's really what you want to do.

#93: What If I Don't Know?

Most of us don't know at 17 or 18 what we want to do for the rest of our lives. It is a good idea to see what is out there before jumping into a degree program.

Some of my friends have even taken time off after high school to explore different career paths before deciding on a major. Another option would be to take general education classes before declaring a major. That way, you can try out different specialized classes and see what you like best.

You can always try different jobs during the summer, when school is out, to give you a good feel for what it's like to work. You may really want to work at someplace but after the summer's done, you find out that it's not for you.

A lot of kids I know take summer jobs to make money. Take advantage of any job training you can because it's the best practice you'll ever get.

Another idea is to talk to a career counselor. You might be perfect for a job you don't even know exists. Talking to a career expert is a good way to find out what is available before settling on something.

#94: Money for School

Even if you're not the smartest kid in your class or the best athlete, there are still quite a few of ways to get money for school. Scholarships are offered for just about anything you can think of. I know a girl who applied for a scholarship for women over six feet tall. I had no idea they offered scholarship money just for being tall!

There are many ways to get money to help with the cost of college. It's just a matter of finding them. Talk to your advisor to point you in the right direction or look online for help. They are going to give the money to someone. Why not you?

#95: Making New Friends

Starting a new school, being away from family, and living on your own for the first time can be overwhelming. It can feel intimidating and lonely. A great way to learn your way around campus and meet new people is to get involved in school activities and groups. Joining a fraternity or sorority can be a great start to gaining a solid support system of friends and gives you a chance to be a leader on campus while being involved in fun and charitable activities.

There are clubs for almost every interest at most schools. The first step is finding something that interests you. Then sign up.

#96: Budgeting

Speaking of money for college, this will be the first time most of us have ever lived on our own. We will have to learn how to budget our money for living expenses. It can be challenging to find the balance between going out and saving money for food.

Most colleges have programs where you can buy food in advance. You can get passes for food on campus and buy them on a month-to-month or per semester basis. That way you won't have to worry about running out of money for food.

Another good tip is to make a list after you have been in school for a few weeks of all the things you spend money on during a week or month. Then you can break it down and see how much money you need for the month. This will help you figure out if you need to cut back on things, so you won't end up broke and hungry by the end of the month.

#97: Laundry

Another thing my friends tell me that is tough about leaving home is doing laundry. Some of them have never washed their own clothes. Here are a few tips they have shared with me:

- There are laundry rooms in most dorm buildings, as well as in other parts of campus. The washing machines generally have some kind of washing instructions on them. A good rule to follow is to wash your clothes in cold water if you don't know what temperature they need. This will also lessen your chances of turning all of your clothes pink.
- After you turn the machine on, let it fill up a little with water before adding a capful of detergent. Then let them mix together before adding your clothes.
- Once they are done, a safe temperature for drying clothes is always low or no heat. Not only does this save energy, it saves your clothes from shrinking. Toss in a dryer sheet to soften your fabrics and

make them come out smelling fresh and clean.

- It is a good idea to do laundry with a friend. This way you have someone to pass the time with while your clothes are getting clean, and you have someone to walk with across campus. You can never be too safe.

#98: Study/Party Balance

Being on our own for the first time can be exciting. I know a lot of people who have a hard time balancing their social calendar with getting to class and finishing assignments.

This is the first time that most of us are away from the watchful eye of our parents. We might be tempted to do things that we would never have done if Mom or Dad was around. No one is perfect but there are small mistakes and there are big ones. The key is to not try something you are not comfortable with and have no control over. Stay away from anything that takes you out of the driver's seat.

Just because we go to college, doesn't mean your life starts and ends there. We only have one shot to make the right choices.

Just remember, if you flunk out of school, the party's over. It's much easier to get into college than to get back into college once you've been asked to leave.

#99: I Changed My Mind

Don't stress if you are in school, on track to one career, and change your mind. People change their majors all the time. You can even switch schools if the one you are attending is not a good fit. Most of your beginning classes are general enough that they can be transferred to another accredited school or degree program.

You don't have to know what you want to do right now and even if you do, you may end up changing your mind after you graduate and step out into a world of new possibilities.

The road-course of life has many twists and turns. The most important thing is to find something that makes you happy and feel good about yourself.

If you find your career interest moving in a different direction, talk to your parents and academic advisor. They can help get you refocused and put you on the right path to a new career.

Ask yourself, what do I love to do? What have I always wanted to do? Know one thing: we can do whatever we put our minds to. I am making my dreams come true every day. The world is yours to discover and I hope to show you that you can do whatever it is you want as long as you stay focused. You may fall off track a few times, but that's why you have your parents and family to help put you right back on your path.

Life really is like a race track; you have to step up to the challenges that lay ahead, knowing full well that any bad mistake can cost you dearly, but once you've arrived at that checkered flag, no one can take away your success.

APPENDIX:

WORKSHEETS

Notes to Self:

Notes to Self:

Notes to Self:

Notes to Self:

Notes to Self:

ABOUT

THE

AUTHORS

ZACH VEACH

16-year-old **Zach "Ziggy" Veach** is a racecar driver for Andretti Autosport in INDYCAR's "Mazda Road to Indy" ladder program in the USF2000 National Championship Series presented by Mazda.

Veach was named to CNN's "Intriguing People" list and has been featured on numerous media outlets including *The Gayle King Show* and on CNN's *Headline News*.

In addition to his racing, Veach is leveraging his youth and unusual occupation as a platform to expose fellow drivers to the dangers associated with driving while distracted, serving as a spokesKID for many programs. He is the developer of urTXT, a Droid application, to fight texting behind the wheel. He is also an advocate for safer driving in conjunction with Oprah Winfrey's "No Phone Zone" and the national spokesperson for *FocusDriven*, an advocacy group for victims of motor vehicle crashes involving drivers using their cell phones. He's even created a safe driving program, Ziggy's Safe Driving, to raise money to give students better training behind the wheel of their street car.

The son of a national truck and tractor-pulling champion, Veach has been racing since age 12; going from go-karts to the cockpit of an open-wheel Formula BMW machine in just 19 months. He was set to start in the Atlantic Championship Series but in early 2010, the series ceased operations. He then signed with Michael Andretti's team, Andretti Autosport: the team with most wins in open-wheel racing. Represented by BRANDed talent agency, Veach, urTXT and "Ziggy's Safe Driving" can all be found online at www.zeachveach.com.

Lindsey Gobel is a freelance author who has been featured in numerous print publications, as well as on the Web. She cowrote another book in the 99 Series with IZOD IndyCar Series driver Sarah Fisher,

LINDSEY GOBEL

titled, <u>99 Things Women Wish They Knew Before Getting Behind the Wheel of Their Dream Job</u>, released May 2010. Lindsey received her bachelor's degree in journalism from Indiana University–Purdue University, Indianapolis, where she earned high honors. She won the 2009 JSO Media Competition award for her profile story on a recovering drug user.

Gobel has a background in marketing and public relations, representing a number of local and national firms. She utilizes her creativity and experience as a journalist to develop innovative marketing concepts, while balancing client goals to manage relationships between advertising partners and the firms she represents. She can be reached at lindsey.gobel@gmail.com.

Available Titles in The 99 Series®

99 Things You Wish You Knew Before...
Facing Life's Challenges
Filling Out Your Hoops Bracket
Going Into Debt
Going Into Sales
Ignoring the Green Revolution
Landing Your Dream Job
Losing Fat 4 Life
Making It BIG In Media
Marketing On the Internet
Speaking In Public
Stressing Out!

99 Things Women Wish They Knew Before...
Dating After 40, 50, and YES, 60!
Getting Behind the Wheel of Their Dream Job
Getting Fit Without Hitting the Gym
Entering the World of Internet Dating
Falling In Love
Planning for Retirement
Starting Their Own Business

99 Things Parents Wish They Knew Before...
Cyberbullying Victimized Their Children
Having "THE" Talk

99 Things Brides Wish They Knew Before Planning Their Wedding

99 Things Teens Wish They Knew Before Turning 16